Blue Watermelon

Mary Freericks

Copyright © 2017 Mary Freericks

All rights reserved.

ISBN: 1974618978
ISBN-13: 978-1974618972

DEDICATION

I would like to express gratitude to my husband, Charley, for all his loving support during my graduate work at Columbia.

Without the help of my son, Charles, this book would not be in your hands.

The cover photo is of the author when she was young and dressed as a flower girl for a wedding that did not take place. The dress she is wearing is a copy of Infanta Margarita Teresa who is in the center of Velazquez's painting entitled "Maids of Honor". Mary's poem, "An Arranged Wedding" refers to this dress.

CONTENTS

Part One

Knots	p. 1
To Hafez	p. 2
Shah Tahmasps's Orders	p. 3
For Forough Farrokhzad	p. 4
My Milk Name	p. 5
Family Album	p. 8
Blue Watermelon	p. 9
Uncle Mesrop	p. 10
The American and the Wooden Doll	p. 11
Don't Let Anyone Kiss You on the Lips	p. 12
Our Garden in Tabriz	p. 16
I'm Moving into this Tree House	p. 18
Blue Kittens	p. 19
At the Landing, a Dare	p. 20
Outhouse in Tabriz	p. 22
American Movies in Tabriz	p. 24
Hot on my Tongue	p. 25
Voski-Babu	p. 28
Our Back Porch	p. 30
The Music Teacher	p. 32
The Thief	p. 33
Carriage Ride	p. 37
Console Radio	p. 39
Kaddakh Mountain	p. 40
The Bombing of Tabriz	p. 42

Part Two

Tastes of Tehran, 1940	p. 47
Home Made Cherry Jam	p. 48
Born into a World of Light	p. 49
The Couch	p. 50
Mekertich's Mother	p. 51
Shushanik's Son	p. 52

Ink	p. 53
Rafik's Dog	p. 55
Piano	p. 56
Piano Lessons	p. 57
Young Girl	p. 58
I was Never Alone on the Streets	p. 59
Walking to School	p. 60
School Doctor	p. 62
Locked Out	p. 63
The Persian Meat Market	p. 64
Around the Pot-Bellied Stove	p. 65
The Voice	p. 68
Woozy in a Taxi	p. 70
In her own Apartment, Tehran	p. 71
H'ramatzek	p. 72
An Arranged Wedding	p. 75
Bulls of Babolsar	p. 78
Cousin Kachik, the Map Maker	p. 79
Prayer	p. 82
Garden Miniatures	p. 83
Small Hotel in Khoramshahr, 1945	p. 87
Ellis Island, 1945	p. 89
Flight	p. 91
Saddi's Ancient Book	p. 94
I Will Rise Up	p. 96

Part Three

Nargiz Mama's Prayer	p. 98
Moving Away	p. 106
Foreign Words and Phrases	p. 114

MARY FREERICKS

Part One

KNOTS

Grind alum and cinnamon, sift light,
as light as the dust of the high hills.
Take lac and female cochineals,
steep the insect bodies four to six
days in the hot sun, stir. In a thin
glass bottle let the rich color settle.
Then strain through two cloths,
add pomegranate rind and iron filings.
Steep the wool in mineral acid and the dye
for thirty-six hours, then boil.

Ready the loom for the hand knotting.
Wind the white cotton warp on rollers.
Through the Persian knots the poem
gathers its shape, a pattern of sound
lifts into a garden. Elk and birds flash.
The white underpinnings stretched taut
on the frame disappear beneath the bright
wool. Only the fringe reveals
the cotton's hidden hold.

MARY FREERICKS

TO HAFEZ

It is hard to start all over. Nothing can moor me now.
The sky is a glass sea I shatter. The turtle is the earth,

not to be endured. I will hold your hand, flowing. Body
to body we are passing through each other.

From its silent tree the nightingale lifts one song.
Ruby throated, the hummingbird has two voices.

Bones weigh me from within, hold down as rocks.
What if I could lift myself, *Meykhane* waits.

The brown snake eats, so slim it can reach the tops
of the narrowest trees. They only give off night carbon.

Neutrinos pass through steel, through the center
of the earth to the other side.

Where is the stained glass window opening to your world?
The pigs are shaking their muddy legs.

There will be more bloodletting. We will abandon
this dry crust of land, the ship that pilots the Milky Way.

Constellations vibrate, their skirts show the underside
of the creature. A cicada darkens my screen.

Is the strident voice a decoy from a needle bill? I feel
six hundred and fifteen year long wings grow on my back.

SHAH TAHMASP'S ORDERS

Disrespect!
Sew up the poet's mouth,
seal him in a jar,
carry to the top of a minaret
and hurl.

The jar shatters;
a curve of snake streaks lightning;
slides into the earth's heart.
A seed of fire from the tongue,

tendrils sprout,
hiss, break the crust.
From Ferdowsi to Farrokhzaad,
word thorns strike the fire of day,

blossom mouths in the night,
a rose garden to test a king.
Come, prick your finger!

MARY FREERICKS

FOR FOROUGH FARROKHZAD, BORN JANUARY 5TH
(The poet killed in a crash, 1967, Tehran)

We were born the same day
in the year of mouths
cradled by the winter sun.

You were the darker sister.
We found each other after your death.
What words can tear off the mountain

that veils your tender skin?
My white grapes weave an arc above you.
I send bees into the honeysuckle of your ears.

Your many voices sprout again:
The acacia blooms, the red star lifts.
I feel your thorn. Our blood mingles.

MY MILK NAME

My name chosen for me, sealed across my forehead
with a cross of oil, a holy name, Mary,
after Mariam Astvatsatsiny and Mary Baker Eddy.

The missionary children around my crib wonder
at doll-like fingers clutching.
My fingers grow, pull across the Persian rug,
Up the mahogany legs, into the butter on the table.

Mama sees the shine of gold in my hair,
calls me, *"Momichka, Dushichka, Lastichka."*
Sews organdy dresses with puffed sleeves,
and ties me up in pink bows, a daughter
after two sons, *"Aghkikjan,"* to my grandparents.

I want to be like the boys, pee from the porch,
Go on walks with Papa on Avenue Ferdusi.
"Change your name to Yram," Leo smiles.
"Tell Papa you're a boy," Peter adds.

I try "Yram," Mary in reverse, on my tongue,
talk Mama into having my head shaved,
at the barber's, see the naked head emerge.

As Yram, I stand in our garden in Peter's sailor suit.
Aunt Vartanoush is momentarily fooled, "Who
is this strange little boy? You haven't introduced me."

"It's our own little Mary," Mama laughs and I blush.
In time my hair grows back thicker
as Mama knew it would.
The watery milk sticks in my throat.
I never thought to look for a milk name of my own.

MARY FREERICKS

At Iraj, my best friend, Nasrin, and the other girls
call me "Mehry." "Mehry, where did you get those
green shoes?" They laugh.

I coax my cousins to let me play soccer
instead of sitting out with the girls.
At a mock wedding, I marry cousin Rafik
with a real ring, "Mary do you take –"

Every Thursday the American soldiers from Camp Amirabad
gather around our upright piano singing,
"You are my sunshine, my only—, Lazy Mary,
won't you get up, Oh it was Mary, Mary, plain
as any name could be, but with propriety, society, Marie—"

I take piano lessons, imagine myself a concert pianist.
The audience claps, presents me bouquets of roses.
Then Papa dies and we move to America.

My cousin Arlene welcomes me to Washington Heights
with chants of "Mary, Mary, my only Mary."
My hair turns brown, shimmering russet.

Shopping at Saks 34th Street, I look at a silky black dress.
"Black is for mourning," Mama shakes her head,
holds up a ruffled eyelet. I pick the siren red.
She reluctantly pays.

Northwestern University at the sorority house
three Marys on the one floor and the phone
ringing, ringing. "Little Mary, phone call for you!"
They tease me when I shed my bra as I reach my room.

BLUE WATERMELON

I marry holding on to the Mary, but lose Avakian,
"Mrs. Freericks," my new boss at the credit union calls,
and I just sit there. "Mrs. Freericks," he calls again,
"Mrs. Freericks," 'til he rouses me to my new name.

"Yes, Sir," I answer.

My husband whispers, "Supping," "Bunny Toes," or
teases "Sapphire." My sons call me "Ma Ma,"
then "Mommy," and now "Mom." "Hey Mom!"
Sometimes they startle me with "M a r y."

And still I search as Scandinavian children search,
fingers in the sand, I feel for a smooth stone,
a white stone to break open to my real name.

MARY FREERICKS

FAMILY ALBUM

Peter and I full front in Mama's album,
I hold a pie plate below my belly button.
He is completely nude caught in black and white
placed between the four corners.
I am two and a half, Peter three or four.
Leafing through the album past Papa
in his big chair, past Harik and Voski
in the center of the family, past Leopold
on his tricycle near the black sheep –
later sacrificed when Vaghoush was discharged
from the Persian Army, friends always stop
and stare at Peter and me, naked.

BLUE WATERMELON

Pistons chug, rods push,
pull away Papa and his promise
of blue watermelon,
leave black smoke.
Mama alone on the platform
as her belly rises
Gasha and Simon comfort her.
She knows her allegiance.
The Soviets will not stamp her passport,
will not, will not, will not, will.
Sing Mama on the train
Moskva, Rostov, the Don River,
The Black Sea, Caucasus.
His son moves in her belly
to the turn of the wheels, Erivan,
the dazzling sky,
Mt. Alavand, Tabriz,

Khosrov, Voski, plums,
pomegranates and Papa's arms.
She watches him carry
each new watermelon. Her young eyes
expect the blue slice
shining on her plate,
as he serves; yet, another red,
the sweet pulp, the seeds. Papa winks.
Between births, her breasts filling,
sing of blue mosques in Persian sun,
and blue ponds in gardens,
goldfish brimming.

When Papa teases and his knife cuts,
she hurls her high heels.
Papa catches her and she
becomes his ballerina. He chants,
Moia zhena, moia zhena, my wife,"
lips on her ears, her neck,
the deep husband kiss:

another son;
a daughter.
Night comes, Papa ill,
and the sky
turns black.

The Atlantic slams its ink
against her Victory Ship.
Mama bargains in broken English
holds my hand at Macy's
the price firm.
At the A&P cut halves
She counts change.
Past the Sunday bachelor
she holds on to Papa's photo,
releases each child
with curved fingers.
Under the swing set
sing of watermelon ripening from seed
as her grandsons ride over it.
The sugar baby splits to my knife,
glistening twin suns of the yellow watermelon,
an alchemy.
Mama holds her breath.
Chest shaking, her mouth pops laughter
unstoppable, eyes over brim.
I serve Mama a slice of sun.
Papa's eyes

BLUE WATERMELON

shine from our faces,
his wink.

UNCLE MESROP

When I was light enough to jump
on Uncle Mesrop's belly as he lay
stretched on the couch, he would
lift me in the air with a laugh.
What a ride as he smiled, lifting me
higher. What a soft landing!

He did not care then about handwriting,
the chicken scratches.
He did not hand me the Palmer method
or show me how to hold a pen
and draw circles, legible letters.

He was all smiles
as I did handstands,
and made circles in the air
with my feet.

THE AMERICAN AND THE WOODEN DOLL

A little man only a foot tall is running
on the floor. I eye the corners of the couch
and lift my feet higher. The creature
is closing in. Might he bite? Is he wild?

My cat could catch him in her mouth
and hold him in the air swinging
like a baby rabbit. The little man is dancing,
lifting shiny blue shoes.

Down on one knee, he sings, "Mary, Mary…"
How does he know my name?
Miniature eyes look into mine.
His arm extends to shake hands.
I blush. At a touch will he shrink me?
I hesitate. Are his feelings hurt?

The little man is shaking my hand.
He is alive.
He bows and is gone.
Why are the grown ups calm?

A wooden doll lies limp on the couch
with crumpled string.
Where is the little man?

MARY FREERICKS

DON'T LET ANYONE KISS YOU ON THE LIPS

Mama warned.
"Tour Inds Me Patrchik," Uncle Vahram
chanted as he pinched my cheek pulling me towards him.
I turned away denying his wet kiss.

The servant girl found me in the morning
on my hands and knees eyeing the cat.

She urged me to the window, climbed on
and squeezed my body with her large legs, rocking.
Her skirt bunched up,
she kept watching as she squeezed my body.
"Don't tell anyone," she warned.

I didn't want to be her horsey.
I was uncomfortable like the cat
when I held her too tight.

My brothers found out about sex
before me, touching forbidden spots.
They were older. The girls in school talked about boys.

Igor, my brother's best friend, watched my schoolmates emerge.
He told my brother, Leo, I was the prettiest.

When we played chess, he held my hand for some time
as he passed me chess pieces. Others were bolder. Let their knees
sidle up to my legs. One Persian boy massaged my palm
with his thumb 'til I felt a tingle
beyond his finger.

BLUE WATERMELON

In a room alone on the second floor
I touched myself on the antique sofa, rocked on the embroidered pillow. Suddenly a man's face appeared in the window.

I jumped. He smiled, wiping the window clean.

MARY FREERICKS

OUR GARDEN IN TABRIZ

Under the sun and shade of fruit trees,
We know our ranks.
Leo is *Paron Hantess*,
Peter, in spite of protests,
Tikin Hantess, and I, the youngest,
a servant. "I want *Tikin Hantess*,
the wife," I argue. "I'm a girl."
My brothers ameliorate.
"You can be ALL the servants."

Fingers in dirt, I pull
the arching flesh of protest.
The agitated worm hangs in the air,
skin blinded by sun, slides down.
I hold tight. I am the giant,
draping worms on my wrist.
I hold my wriggling bracelet up.
"Dirty things!" Mama screams,
"Take them away!"

My brothers dig a mud hole deeper,
divert more water from our stream.
I take off my Sunday shoes and socks
for two *shahies*. I lift
my organdy dress and sink
up to my knees in muddy water,
slosh up and down. My brothers laugh.
Mud squishes between my toes.
Mama grabs me. Her rapid spanks smart
before I can open my mouth.

BLUE WATERMELON

Out of earshot we chant,
The clever King.
The stupid Queen.
"Khelok Takavor.
Heemar Takoohi."
The clever King takes us fishing.

On my three-wheeler I follow
the two wheelers around
and around the pond, turn
with my brothers towards the outhouse.
No railing guards the sunken bluestone
beneath the porch. My three wheeler bumps.
Unbalanced, head first I hit.
Mama comes running,
gathers me up.

MARY FREERICKS

I'M MOVING INTO THIS TREE HOUSE

I don't remember
climbing
as a child
just hugging trees

with legs curled
around the trunk
pulling myself up
sliding down

as my brothers called
from above
how I envied their height
the view from the top

BLUE KITTENS

Behind the chicken coop my brothers
whisper, "She drowned them."
"All of them?"

"All of them."
"Even the three pink,
and the rare blue?"

"The servant girl carried the pot."
I imagine the struggle, Voski
holding each kitten down,

the small body resisting,
turning limp in her hand. No!
My brothers are fibbing.

The cat is still pregnant.
Kittens are white to black,
not pink or blue.

I search the dark corners,
open closet doors. The cat
comes out, half her size.

I find no kittens.
Voski with the voice of many orchards,
how did she drown them?

I want to dig them up,
blow air into their tiny lungs,
see the pink fur, the blue eyes.

MARY FREERICKS

I find no mound.
Are my brothers telling lies or
could Voski kill?

BLUE WATERMELON

AT THE LANDING, A DARE

Halfway up the stairs Harik's hunting guns
hang. Leo finds the glass door unlocked.
He pulls a gun down, aims. Is he
play acting? Peter dodges unashamed.

The scene unclear I start the climb.
Leo swivels, catches my temple,
with the barrel. "Don't move."
Peter's voice wobbles, "Get down."

Is the gun loaded? Will a bullet cut…
Would my own brother pull the trigger?
"Stand still to prove you trust me."
Stubborn or brave, I stand my ground.

Leo cocks the trigger, the click.
We are play acting in a game.
that is dead serious. I hold my breath
against the blast.

In that moment the adult trust
falters. The oncoming tragedy
the woman wills at any cost to alter.
The little sister raises her eyes

lifts above the barrel into Leo's.
A smile crosses his face.
He drops the barrel,
"Now I know you love me."

MARY FREERICKS

OUTHOUSE IN TABRIZ

We watch from the porch,
the rising pile two men shovel
from our outhouse. Piles rolled up,
they work steadily as if
they are shoveling coal.
One wipes his face with the back
of his hand, smiles up.

Held by that scene, the smell,
we stand a long time.
My brothers tease, "You'll be one
when you grow up, a shovel
in your hand."
"No, you, shit all over your arms."
In our fear of this, the lowliest
job, we dread and admire these men,
their thin bodies, their prowess,
their surprising smiles.

The mound doubles, the men, up to their ankles,
shovel six months of our living in this ritual,
excrement from grandparents, uncles, aunts,
mother, father, cook, two maids, and guests.
There is no singling whose prize
as all mingles indistinguishable
into one mountain.

When we sat on the cool steps
leading to the school cellar,
Nassrin told me jinns, with long arms,
half animal, half human, tunnel
with claws deep underground.

BLUE WATERMELON

More than the spider or scorpion
curling its tail, I feared a jinn
inside the hole. I crouched uneasy
in the outhouse dreading a long hairy arm,
the claws that might reach up and grab me.

With their shovels these men might dislodge
one. I watch the pile for movement,
a disturbed jinn with its apelike body
jumping out, reaching to drag a man down.

MARY FREERICKS

AMERICAN MOVIES IN TABRIZ

"The witch is scary with sharp teeth."
My brothers talked me out of seeing *Snow White*.

But my parents took me to *The Phantom of the Opera*,
I saw the scars on his burned face. Trembling

watched his hand saw the chain of the chandelier.
When I hear Chopin's Prelude

I see the man cough up blood
onto the piano keys.

BLUE WATERMELON

HOT ON MY TONGUE

Spi moladetskaia moia prekransia.
Sleep my beautiful baby.
Mama sings in Russian.
Byoushki, bayhou, bayhou

Lavash from Papa hot on my tongue
out of the smoking *tonir*,
into my mouth rolls
the Armenian word.

At the dinner table when
not even pidgin comes
into my four-year-old head,
no words for the image,
my short arms part.
With fists I form my own words,
"Booroomeh, Kazane."

Papa, Mama,
Harik and Voski,
my brothers all bewildered
look back.
My words splash down as pebbles.
Their wild colors under water
no one recognizes,
and my arms close.

"*Aghkikjan,*" Harik says, "Wait.
The right words will come."

Sangak, thick Persian bread
pulled from the hot bricks,
baleh, chashm, I now decipher

my friend Nasrin as she confides
in Farsi her games
with the Princess at Gulestan Palace.

Khodah hafez, faces leave.
The twin engine plane takes us,
a ship waits in the Gulf,
Arab boatmen, American sailors,
new tongues. My own rehearses
new shapes. *Atalakan Kaaki,* Wonder
Bread, hello and kiss.
"John wants to kiss you."

But when I fall
an early language as a broken bone
cuts through the flesh
its jagged edge protrudes.

We are all receivers.
Our tongues tasting new words,
naming in many tongues the same
chair, but how can I name
that feeling on the brink,
my nostrils open to the smell,
how to shape the letters?
Images fly
as a green-breasted bird,
not in the "Field Guide."

English surfaces, the rest
mingle in a cavern under
the tongue as fireflies.
The finite words stop.
The cave grows dark.
No words come.
I make fists.

BLUE WATERMELON

Under my tongue
the white stone locked.

VOSKI-BABU

"*Aghkikjan*, go in, find some eggs."
A sputter of straw, a flutter of wings,
the rooster, the hens watch my fingers
sneak under their bellies. I find
one egg. Voski scolds the hens.

Hair pure white, face radiant,
in her long black dress, she walks slowly.
Arms full of puppies, I follow.
She reaches for peaches,
bends to me.

The egg man crouches on our porch,
two baskets filled with eggs.
Voski selects. I lower into the pot
of water. I am the tester,
catch the rotten eggs that float back.
Voski rejects. The egg man rubs
his stubby face. A smoky smile
breaks to her acumen.

At thirteen Harik's bride,
she came with a doll under her arm.
Her mother-in-law pulled it
away. "You are a *harss*,
not a child." Harik was thirty-five.

BLUE WATERMELON

A stillbirth, then two daughters
lost in the fire, Voski wore black,
a child herself.
But her sons came all healthy,
Alexan, Phoghos,
Vaghinak, Vaghoush,
four sons, Harik satisfied.

In the years they held each other,
signals of growing close,
a touch of the hand, the rivalry of cards,
every evening the shuffling, the dealing,
the melds, a wink at me when she won.

The sons bring brides.
Grandchildren multiply.
Skein winds around my wrist
over the cat's stretching paw
into a ball in Voski's hand.
Wool whirlpools, trickles
to a tickle, ends. Released,
I climb into her full lap.

Stringing grapes, preserving, baking,
the household vibrates to her lead,
harsses all in tune.

My brothers and I open her drawer
and take the white pills. We think
they are candy and stuff our mouths.
We spit and spit the bitter quinine.

Mama reads from the Bible. Voski listens,
nods approving. "I want to die
before Grandpa," she says. "Dear God,
let me be first."

MARY FREERICKS

OUR BACK PORCH

The metal edge of the potty digs
into my fanny. My feet on the Persian rug,
I sit waiting; Mama urges me on.

Leo and Peter pee from the porch.
I watch who can aim higher,
arcs of yellow through the railing.
I try; wetness drops down my legs,
a failure.

I climb the stairs holding Mama's hand.
Tikin Khanazadian waits on the landing.
I let go, watch Mama leave.
The other children take me in.

Mama warns me not to repeat what I said.
I like the words. I let go again.
Why is she so angry? She locks me
inside the closet. In the dark
I feel for the door. Nothing opens.
I kick and kick crying, "Let me out!"
I feel the wetness down my leg,
the closed in tightness.

I see the light as she opens the door
and takes me, wet, in her arms.
"I didn't know. I would never
lock you in. All you had to do
was turn the knob."
I refuse elevators, climb six, seven
flights. When brakes squeal
and the subway stops in a black tunnel,
lights flickering,

BLUE WATERMELON

I am back in that dark closet.

And when Mama loses sight,
our bathroom becomes her dark closet,
she palms the walls, cannot find the door,
and she panics, pushing, pushing.
All the time the door is open.

MARY FREERICKS

THE MUSIC TEACHER

We are on the steps of the children's orchestra
ready for a group portrait. I hold the flag
draped across my knee since I play no instrument.
The plump boy next to me sits back so the pole
will not poke him. Others hold violins lowered,
bows over one knee. A drum centers Leo's head.
He wears short pants. Peter is on my step
At the opposite end, his feet crossed at the ankles.

Paron, you were so easy with your hands,
grabbing a child in the crotch, fingering
his flute. The wet kiss on my lips
if you could catch my face between both your hands,
you loved orchestrating all the sweet organs.

You are smiling, proud of your musicians.
How can you tune them? This is our moment.
As the photographer watches, you cannot grab
any of us, or goose. Violins protect vital organs.
We are safe now, my lips and face dry from spit
as the slow camera tightens its long focus.

THE THIEF

The daughter I never had
wakes
     crying with fear.
How can I comfort her?
     Alone in the house
     I shiver.

What can I tell her
of courage?
     I wrap the blanket
around us. I am a child
     asleep in Tabriz.
     The thief at the window

bends the metal bars and
enters.
     Voski catches him
in the dark, her hands
     on his throat.
     I see the struggle

from behind Mama. The men wake,
Harik, Papa.
     They grab Voski,
not the thief, pull at her arms
     as she holds on
     to that throat.

I lie stiff. A hunchback
enters
    my nightmares,
Mama takes me in her arms.
    sings, *"Moomichka."*
    Her breath tenses.

She is a girl in Russia,
Bolsheviks
    on the stairs,
a knock on the door,
    someone taken
    to be shot.

The Atlantic Ocean rising,
three women
    on the cargo ship,
no, two. I am only a girl.
    The hurricane hits.
    We cannot lock the cabin,

Captain's orders. The ship filled
with sailors.
    Their muscles bulge
under cotton sleeves.
    Even the whisper
    "rape," terrifies.

A six-foot-four young man
picks me up
    at Walgreen's over
strawberry soda.
    What if he's
    an ex-convict?

BLUE WATERMELON

Mama serves Campbell's soup hot
with her fears.
    But I wear his matching sweater
and we roll away on skates.
    She cannot lock
      the cabin door.

In the subway a man
unzips.
    Mama and I against
our seats tense.
    The penis hangs,
      the prune balls.

On Tenth Avenue a man walks,
a knife
    in his hand,
snaps out the blade.
    I hold my mother in my lap.
    She has no teeth.

I have no daughter.
My sons
    sleep in the next room breathing.
Alone in the double bed
    I turn to the
    empty side.

Without my husband's heat
I cannot
    fall asleep.
I hear footsteps creaking
    in the hall.
    I shudder.

I call for the strength in Voski's
hands.
    My oldest son wakes
crying. I brave the dark hall,
    lift his warm body
    against mine.

His breath is short,
face red.
    "What is it?
A nightmare?"
    "The Queen of Evil,
    eyes all over her body."

He sees her face peering in the
window.
    I wipe this dirt.
I see Voski, her hands on the throat.
    They pull her off.
    Saved by the men

the thief's lungs fill. In the gaslight we see
the face,
    our servant's son.
Voski's hands shake. "But why?"
    "Bread for my mother."
    "I would have gladly given."

My son falls asleep. There is no
intruder.
    My daughter slips into my dream.
A three-eyed man stalks us.
    Her hands are soft.
    Her hands are lethal.

BLUE WATERMELON

CARRIAGE RIDE

The whip, the tail of the horse lifts.
Peter is holding the reins.
The gelding in blinders turns.
How did he cajole the driver?
I want a chance.

Safe between Papa and Mama I am stuffed
in the back seat against leather.
The driver is teaching my brother
left and right past the silver shops
the smell of roasting beets.
The huge horse obeys.
In the open Peter is in charge.
I envy his ease.
We begin the climb. A carriage wheel
wobbles. Will Peter manage the steep rise?
We must go four handed up the precipice.
Slowing through the pass, we reach
a village. They come out and point,

a mother in a soiled shawl,
a baby wrapped in cotton at her breast.
The other two children pull at her arms.
They are pointing. The dark boy
is pointing at me.

"Your organdy dress, your curls,"
Mama assures. "They take you
for Shirley Temple." But she knows
they have never seen a movie.
I touch my curls.

In the meadow the driver lets go.
Peter is on his own. We rush headlong.
The horse shies, will not stop
at Peter's weak pull. I am on the horse
galloping away, shaking off the burden
of carriage. Peter's thin arms cannot hold
us back. The driver is pulling,
reining me in, leather straps squeezing
the wind out of my lungs. With a jolt
the carriage bumps my back and I am still.

I am running in a field of poppies,
sedum, and borage with Papa.
We stop and I pick a handful for Mama.

Riding back I want to hold the reins,
but Peter is sitting next to the driver.
When do I get my turn?
The horse lifts its tail, balls of golden
shit my revenge.

BLUE WATERMELON

CONSOLE RADIO

A glass of water brims, my pass
to Papa's lap, his arms open.
I climb aboard. The radio is dead.

We turn the dial. No breath comes,
all the tubes dark, the voices
mute. The chest stands stiff.

Papa's head in the cabinet,
he extracts tubes. I dust.
The ten second wait,

coils glow with orange blood
of giant insects. The long test,
two burnt out tubes remain dark,

replaced, the console lights up,
all the tungsten lyres tuned.
Negative current oscillates.

The vacuum tubes resonate.
The one voice, Hitler's.
Papa's shoulders tremble me.

He turns the dial.
From every station,
Sieg Heil! Sieg Heil!

Our radio has lost its many voices.
Our radio wears Hitler's lungs.
I will stab the speaker.

KADDAKH MOUNTAIN

Half awake, I hear Peter and Leo.
Harik takes them on his hunting trip.
As I fall asleep
they reach Kaddakh Mountain.

Harik raises his shotgun.
Mountain goats scamper.
A partridge in mid-flight
plunges.

Gun smoking, Harik slips the prey
into his game bag.
Sees a poisonous snake
slither towards my brothers.

A blast! The snake's head
splatters. Its body writhes
near the boys' legs.

Harik drags it to the carriage
floor. When they reach home
he buries the body in our yard.

I dream of the headless snake
moving underground.
What else is hidden down there alive?

Harik oils a cotton swab,
Slips the rod into each barrel.
He knows the worth of these guns.

BLUE WATERMELON

A trace of burned powder fills my nostrils.
Hitler's *Sieg Heils* shake
Papa's console radio.

MARY FREERICKS

THE BOMBING OF TABRIZ

My brothers' violin lessons stopped
by bombs! Leo lifts his bow.
Machine gun answers from below.

"Billiard balls hitting,"
Paron Assatour explains. Again,
"Blow outs. Truck tires,"
tunes the violin.

Peter runs to the window.
White dots roar.
Leo is at the window.
We are all at the window,
watching wings.

The door opens.
Papa home midday,
Bazaar closed, buzzing.
"Marand! They hit Marand!"

"Hit the women, the children?"
"Mistook tents of vacationers
for military."

Harik gathers papers,
Burns all, buries something.

BLUE WATERMELON

We move into basement
down big steps,
huddle in unfinished room.
Servants set up beds
as light from narrow window
dims. Harik strikes a match.
We sit quiet,
Listening…

Roaring toward us a bomber.
Mama whisper screams,
"Blow it out. They'll see us."

In the dark, I hold my breath.
The bomber lowers over our roof.
Mama's hand tightens.

Leo still in her belly,
she left Russia.
Those communists now tearing
our Tabriz skies.
The roof buzzed, our house shakes.

In the silence between bombs,
"Tell us a story," Harik asks.
Papa starts, his voice holding us
In the dark, "A Persian woman, young,
pretty, was told to marry an older man,
and so she did, but as fate would have it,
she fell in love with a young man.
They found them together in the very act.
The husband saw with his own eyes.
Accused of adultery, she was taken…"

A squadron of bombers!
"prisoner. Caught in the act, she
was sentenced to die,
taken as she struggled up
the many steps of the Arc."
The fortress two blocks from our house,
a bomb hit, bounced off.

"At the top, her head covered,
her screams muffled, walked to the edge,
pushed off. As she fell
her *chador* opened as if
a parachute.
She landed on her feet.
'An omen from Allah.'
They let her go."

Listening to the light in Papa's voice,
I let go… fall into sleep
think if ever accused,
if ever taken to a high tower,
I will wear a full skirt,
carry an umbrella,
open it,
float down,
land.

In the dark basement for two nights
with each bomb reverberating
I imagine my death.

BLUE WATERMELON

At dawn we go upstairs
find Russian soldiers patrolling
our dirt street, young, light-haired boys.
Mama forgets her fears, calls out
through the bars of our window,
"Zdravstvuyzte!"
The young man lowers his gun,
blue eyes smiling up.
"Ya Maskvitchkaya," one after the other
they chime. Mama talks...
of the best borscht. Other soldiers
gather, look up at their native tongue
in the strange Azerbaijani city.

I stay quiet. How can she talk
to those communists?
She turns to me, "They're only boys."

Part Two

BLUE WATERMELON

TASTES OF TEHRAN, 1940

A saucer of cream off the top of the milk, I push back
the wrinkled skin. Harik leans close. I take a taste.
He takes over. My brothers and I dip lettuce into rose water,
the sweet crunch. Makhmood brings *madzoon apour*,
the yogurt soup hot in my mouth. The roast lamb gone,
I suck the lamb bone 'til marrow propels into the back
of my mouth. Peter and I pull the wishbone, a slippery tug.
He pulls harder, the bone cracks and breaks. He wins.
We lick our fingers, see no one is watching, toss the bones.

Fruit piled high in silver servers in the garden,
ladyfinger grapes green as water jewels, plums, peaches,
and pomegranates. Papa slices through the tough skin,
a beehive of berries in rows. The juice squirts
in my eye. I take a tangy bite, spit out thin pits.
I pull a fig off our fig tree, sink my teeth into the sweet
depth, swallow pits and all, catch a cherry, eat
around the pitted half, use the juicy cup to color my lips.

MARY FREERICKS

HOMEMADE CHERRY JAM

Asked to help, a man reaches up for the heavy
ceramic jar on the top shelf of the pantry,
loses his balance. The jar topples
grazes his head, spills jam.

Khourik hurries with wet linen towels.
Wipes red from his bald head.

Mama screams. You've ruined
our homemade jam, the Persian rug!

Embarrassed, I watch
the jagged scar emerge.
He smiles a sheepish smile.

BLUE WATERMELON

BORN INTO A WORLD OF LIGHT

Born into a world of light
schooled by Zoroastrian
sun worshippers,
under a brilliant Persian sky,
I need windows all around me.

MARY FREERICKS

THE COUCH

No one is in the room,
not Khourik, not Mama,
not a servant. I climb my mount,
get into the rhythm, jump
higher and higher on the couch.

The cabinet bangs my head.
I turn and see the clock.
The pendulum swings no accusing finger
in its steady shine. I rub my head.
Did Mama see? Is she running
to spank me?

Mother Armenia looks down from the Kerman
on the wall. Her head rests on the hand.
Clouds of red wool do not collide in anger
above Mount Ararat. The sword rests
on the sand at her bare feet.
I do not know of massacres, or broken columns,
do not recognize the destroyed cities
that surround her: Sis, Gharin, Van.

My fingers trace her mandolin.
Her dress glows golden as sunset
unfolding on a lake.
Her hair is my sky. I am out of reach
of Mama's anger. I step away
from the clock cabinet and jump
with abandon. Mother Armenia winks
our secret.

MEKERTICH'S MOTHER

The oldest woman I knew was keen at ninety-nine.
They said she could see better than a twenty-year old
and had all her own teeth. She was small,
draped in a black silk shawl, skin wrinkled
her eyes as an infant's blue again, she could bite an apple.
Mama sketched the shawl draped around her head
and clear eyes. We sat around her,
waiting for her to speak.

MARY FREERICKS

SHUSHANIK'S SON

My cousin in a wheelchair makes guttural sounds.
His hand travels from his arm.
I hold on to Mama.

Shushanik shakes her head, "He had a terrible fright.
He was fine until that day, strong and healthy."
He is old enough to shave.
What could frighten someone so?

They will not tell me about his best friend,
a Russian officer in Rostov, or the spies
hired to kill him.
I imagine a dark cave, a skeleton.

But it was morning. Shushanik's son
was taking the garbage out. He was fine
until he lifted that lid, in the bin a body,
shot. He turned the head, his best friend.
He screamed. He could not stop screaming.

He kept on screaming for days.
His legs and arms gave way.
He became closed in a box of flesh.

BLUE WATERMELON

INK

1. Tehran

The teacher's voice drones.
My desk sprouts fingers;
stems of sea plants wiggle
from the hole for the inkwell.
An ocean rises within me.

The teacher steals up the aisle,
out of sight, a column
stretches an arm.

My cheek stings
as if hit by hot sand.
Tears blur. I wrench my hand
out of the hole. My arms
slide into my lap.

Mama goes straight to the *Modir*
Gives her a hand painted Easter egg
with a Czarina on one side.

The scolded teacher stands over me,
"Why did you, TELL, your mother?"
Her coal eyes sizzle.
I ready myself for another slap,
but she folds her arms down,
makes fists.

Guilt and anger root
in my missing mouth.

2. Washington, D.C.

Miss Powell is not my boss, but
she catches me entering the Old
Belasco Theater early from lunch,
before I take off my coat,
"Run these off!"

I find the handle. The slit
on the cylinder opens.
I crank faster and faster. The last
sheet has no letters only blue dots.
I stop cranking.

Miss Powell stands, her huge frame
over me.
"The mimeo stopped working," I falter.
She lifts a golden bottle above me.
"Ink," she shouts,
"I, N, K, INK!"

I start walking.
"Where are you going?"
she screams. I keep walking
up the stairs.
Her face gets redder and smaller
with each rise.

RAFIK'S DOG

If the door unlatches, the fiend will charge out,
huge body in the air, teeth bared.
Why do my cousins keep that dog,
a wild German Shepherd sired by a wolf?

I am too young for Agnes and Mano's girl talk.
I follow the boys far from the tearing at the leash,
the chains, the incessant barks and growls.

"But you're only a girl."
I convince my cousins to let me play.
My lucky day, I kick the soccer ball, a goal.

I do not see the dog knock Agnes down,
his teeth at her throat.
They cannot pull the beast off.

I see her all bandaged lying in bed.
They whisper of rabies shots and her luck
they finally pulled him off
before those teeth reached her trachea
or the jugular.

She can hardly talk for the pain.
I watch Agnes's eyes.
Why do they keep that dog?

MARY FREERICKS

PIANO

Inside the piano there is a harp.
The angels are hiding
under the black lid.
They play with soft drums.
They listen to my fingers
as I touch the ivory
they resonate.

The piano tuner plucks the strings
one by one. He tightens
the loose ones.
The angels hover.
He listens to the tuning fork
'til the strings salute.

PIANO LESSONS

"You don't even look at him.
You are so proud.
You stand with your back to him
as you hand him your music,"
Mama smiles.
She has trained me right.
But I know the Armenian boy hired
as a servant to take me
to piano lessons, he
stands behind me.

I hand him my music without looking
into his large brown eyes.
We sit silently on the bumpy bus
up the *Khiaban* not touching,
his hand on his knee so close to me,
his curly head high.

I lead up the steps.
"Curve your fingers," Madame Afanasian
scolds. "You must practice scales."
My fingers silver under water
gather the swoop of melody.
Flying fish wink.

On the bus back his long lashes lift.
My head fixes straight ahead,
his dark eyes cover me, and the whistle
of my heart flickers to his breath.

MARY FREERICKS

YOUNG GIRL

She is on the edge of the bed
sitting up, legs together,
arms folded across the pubic hairs,
hiding what she can, but hands open,
pretending not to hide.

Her eyes are wide,
the shoulder bone protrudes,
breasts barely curved.
There is a shadow behind her.
Her toes dig into the rug.

Soon she will lie down
on the white sheet
and cover herself with the green
blanket. The dream waits to enter
as the body she shapes climbs the stairs.

I WAS NEVER ALONE ON THE STREETS

Mama held my hand up the stairs to *Tikin* Khnazadian's nursery school
   in Tabriz. One day she was late. I waited and waited 'til every child left. I
   was alone, but for the teacher. Tears welled up. I heard Mama.
"Don't cry, *Dushichka,* I was only a little late. You know I will
always come for you." She dried my tears.

In kindergarten in Tehran, Mama walked me back and forth to school
   holding my hand as we crossed the Avenues.

At Shiraz, the Zoroastrian girls' school, Mama took me to enroll.
She entrusted me to walk with one or both of my brothers.
They dropped me off and went off to the boys' school of shaved heads.

Once Leopold forgot to pick me up. I watched the girls leave
in groups and one by one as parents or caretakers picked them up.
I tried to go on my own, but the custodian blocked my way.
"You have to wait," he said.
I got scared. I should have left earlier when he wasn't watching.
What if Leo never comes?

WALKING TO SCHOOL

I am too angry after a fight
with my brothers I cannot remember.
I walk ahead. Leo is supposed to walk me
to school, or Peter. I am not to go alone.
I rush ahead, step out into the street.
A man speeding on his bicycle strikes me down.
I fall backwards, head against the pavement.
"He hit her and ran."
Adults form a circle above me
Whisper as if I am not there.
"How could he leave her lying in the middle
of the street?"

Someone is lifting me. I hear Leo's voice,
feel his arms hard under my armpits.
He tells Igor to carry our books.
I cannot see them as if night has fallen
like a *chador* down to my ankles.
My feet abandoned dangle in sun.
I watch them hanging as if I have no body.
They are birds migrating without a flock
to lead them. They have bows in their heads
like clowns, toe, heel, toe, heel.
Soon they will somersault.
These are not my feet,
wearing my shoes.
I have no body.
I am all armpits
cut by Leo's bony arms.
Home is so far.
We will never reach.

BLUE WATERMELON

Mama sits over me changing compresses
but I am not there. Night passes.
She lifts another compress.
My eyes open to her hand
over me like a white bird.

"Moomichka!" You were gone so long.
I thought you would never return.
I prayed. Now you are back,
promise you will never leave."

SCHOOL DOCTOR

I am the shortest in the class,
but make my way to the end
of the line. We are waiting
for the eye hook to lift the lid,
a test for trachoma.
I watch the other children.
The metal instrument clamps
on the eye.
The line dwindles to two girls
ahead of me, then one.
I run.
The teacher catches me,
calls the *Modir*.
Together they hold me.
The doctor lowers the eye hook;
cold metal enters.
The lid rolls up
as if he is turning my eye
inside out. They scold.
"You should be ashamed."

BLUE WATERMELON

LOCKED OUT

I knock on the locked door.
My knocks muffled by the garden wall.
No one can hear me inside our house.
I am locked out.

I cry louder. Why can't Mama hear me?
Where are the servants?
My fist hurts from knocking.
In tears I kick the door.

The family living in a garage
watch me, the poor rich girl.
The mother holding her infant,
the son and daughter holding her skirt.

I am jealous of their closeness.
The mother breast feeds. The grandmother
walks to the ditch washes fruit and the babies behind.
I knock again and cry out. A huge camel watches me.

Gets too close. I kick and kick the door.
The door swings open. I nearly fall through.
Shout at the servant, "Where were you?"
I want to beat him with fists as I hide my tears.

THE PERSIAN MEAT MARKET

1.

I hold Papa's hand as we pass the carcasses.
My stomach turns. We brush off flies.
The butcher greets us. Papa points to the best leg of lamb.
In the darkened stall the butcher unhooks the carcass.
Papa chats as the butcher weighs and chops.
Wipes blood on his apron. The bargain made
hands Papa the wrapped packages.

2.

No place for a woman, Makhmoud, our cook,
did the marketing. Once, caught in a riot, pushed and pulled,
by the crowd, his food grabbed from his hands,
clutching the empty basket, he ran so fast he could not
get his breath. Face white, hands shaking he arrived
home. Khourik administered valerian to calm him.

3.

At the A&P the butcher hides behind the wall.
Antiseptic lights shine on the Saran Wrapped meat.
The price stamped, no bargaining. Women
peer through the wrapping, fill their baskets, pay.

AROUND THE POT-BELLIED STOVE

The gas lamp shines on Boris's dark hair and bold military buttons.
Mama questions. He answers freely, "My sister Goharik is fine." I feel his
    ring, the Masonic symbols carved in onyx.

Mama says, "I hear you held Stalin's coat." Boris tells us, "I was afraid
      to.
They might think I'm hiding a bomb under a sleeve and jump me."

Mama asks about the Big Four Conference in Tehran.
Boris is silent.
"Did you translate for Stalin in English?" She continues to question.
Boris remains silent as if a glass wall has frozen between us.

I am uneasy as Mama continues her questions, "or Russian for
    Roosevelt?"
An awkward imbalance of questions with no answers.
His face wears the same smile. Our cave of curiosity
deepens. Boris is silent.

My lids grow heavy, narrow on the gas flame, dark all around.
Mama changes the subject, "Bed time."

Boris finds his voice, "Good night, Mary."
Opens his arms.
He is my cousin again.

MARY FREERICKS

A MISSIONARY BIRTHDAY PARTY

Stew meat hidden under the gravy
I take small bites, cut the fat off.
The birthday boy, David, shoots peas
catapulting from his spoon. Guests shoot back.

The butler clears the table.
All the plates gone but my icky stew.
David blows out candles.
All the children get cake but me.

I sit with my stew.
The butler, the maid watch me.
A piece of fat slides down my throat.
I will not take another bite.

I watch the cake. The yellow icing,
the blue flowers
disappear. Children slide from their seats
and run to play.

I am alone at the empty table.
The butler whispers to the maid.
They take the stew away.
A slice of cake appears.

I gulp the sweet cake to catch up with the others.
Where have they gone?
I find them near the ping pong table.
The game over. They are awarding prizes.

David cuts an extra Necco
for the rest of us. I grab. Slip one pink one
into my mouth. The strange taste

BLUE WATERMELON

of America melts on my tongue…

MARY FREERICKS

WATCHING MAMA DRESS

Mama pulls on a girdle,
nets her new hairdo,
arms struggle as her silk dress
wrestles down.
I wait for her head to emerge.

Her face tightens
as she plucks her eyebrows.
Drawers open,
powder puffs,
jewel boxes.

She slips on her emerald ring,
a filigreed bracelet,
lets me twist the gold screw,
adds a diamond necklace.

Drapes a white ermine wrap
across her shoulders,
black tails dance. I run my fingers
through the fur.
She pushes my hand down.
"No, they are sticky."
As papa takes her away.

THE VOICE

In the lacquered box silkworms
bite mulberry leaves, scale the mountain.
Peter and I add handfuls,
cover their white bodies.

After Lily Pons sings
Soldiers clap en masse at Amirabad,
the bravos, and her pure encore
trills in our ears.

Peter throws his head back
a raw egg at his mouth,
albumin rumored to raise
the higher range.
Daily he tests his scale
"la, la, laaa!"

And the silkworms with each molt
enlarging, wiggle through
the stemwork. I stand still.
A white head bridges my hand from
Peter's. Segments tickle.

"The silkworms are gone."
From his practice room Leo
cannot separate our soprano voices.
He looks at the miniature eggs.
"The worm is hiding inside.
You better steam them
or the worm will tear out,
ruin your silk thread."

In a few days the lid springs
silk moths to Peter's touch.
White wings lift and lower
on the piano keys.

"Leopold," Peter's voice cracks,
spills a deepening sun.
Leo laughs, "You'll never sing
like Lily Pons. Your vocal cords
are getting thicker."
Peter stares.

The silk moths live three days.
Empty cocoons, torn, remain
in a lacquered box.

WOOZY IN A TAXI

We are moving up the hill.
Our family is in the back,
a stranger sits on the front seat.
The hard-boiled egg and smell of gas
churn. Mama's handkerchief is too small,
too flimsy. I cannot
hold back the trajectory of my vomit
through my wet fingers,
the sticky smell as it lands
on the back of the man
all over his jacket.
Mama tries to wipe it off, and off my face,
but there is too much.
His new jacket ruined,
he turns around
with a smile.

MARY FREERICKS

IN HER OWN APARTMENT, TEHRAN, 1942

Asaa does not move in with her sister and brother-in-law,
does not take in sewing like Valentina,
does not find a husband to please like Rosa.

No new hairdos, no painted toenails,
no tight silk dresses revealing the divide
between ample breasts.

Her voice rises loud,
harsh tones grate,
rocks of men yield to her blueprints.

We visit her lab,
a wealth of white rabbits in mesh cages.
She pushes back the lid. My hands slip into angora,

soft like Rosa in her silk bathrobe,
soft like Valentina's accepting smile.
Another visit, Asaa in her starched lab coat. Are they

the same white rabbits, all new,
the same red eyes I recognize,
the same soft fur I stroke?

They are calm in these cages,
rabbits with burning eyes,
like the ruby buttons, hard in Valentina's hands,

or the sweet cherry drops
in Rosa's sliver dish,
I politely refuse again and again.

H'RAMATZEK

I join the circle of hands
the youngest at five.
Khourik, my great aunt, makes room,
Voski Babu's place passes
on to me in this circle of women.
Fingers in dough, her hand on mine,
we pat down, shape my first *ketah*.
My diamond
cookie joins the others in
ovens baking. Aroma bleeds
through centuries.

From the ark stranded on Mt. Ararat
women come forth, lift flour
make dough, aroma
of *lavosh* bleeds through Armenia, Asia Minor
into Russia. As our family flees
Turks on a freight train to Salmast.
On to Tabriz, later flee communist bombs,
arrive in Tehran, flour settles.

Spread grape leaves, stuffed
with lamb and rice, lift the tip.
"Roll tighter," Khourik directs.
In the lemon broth battered
by waves boiling all 'round
as families pressed in circles,
my *dolma* holds.

And the aroma in all the houses
those alive and those in memories
of children grown and grandchildren
from Rostov to L.A. Armenian women
in circles braid
dough, braise lamb, wait
as we wait for Papa and Harik to come
home from the bazaar, from dealing
with merchants in Kermans, Hamadans, Herizes,
all knotted with small hands.

My brother's hands carry me under each arm
after the bicyclist knocked me down
and I fainted, I wake to Mama's hand
on my forehead. The same hands
pressing cold compresses
sustained Papa as he tossed delirious.

And hands waiting for Papa
beyond the bright light
as he slipped through ours.

We cross the Atlantic. Leave Khourik.
Break the chain of hands.

Torn from this circle of hands,
Mama in Nyack cooks alone,
holds off teaching me hamburgers,
rushes lessons a month
before my marriage.

BLUE WATERMELON

Alone in Urbana I face
the frozen meat
as my husband inspects the tracks.
Without the circle of women
without the honey, the nutmeats,
the banter, my stomach rises
as I hold raw breasts
of chicken thawing on my palm.

Khetoom, the night before Easter
at Elik's, I sense again this circle
of hands, slim hands of daughters
and daughters-in-law, a wreath of hands
leading from kitchen to table
and back again.

Aroma of pilaf lifts me to birthdays at Berjuhy's,
Christmases at Goharik's, vacation at Gehan's, *kefta*,
kebobs, *lahmajunes*, and *lavash* as they sprinkle dough.
Mothers, daughters, grandmothers, aunts, and cousins

Around the table rolling dough, a flowered wreath
of hands from kitchen to table feed each other.

MARY FREERICKS

AN ARRANGED WEDDING

            To Velazquez and the "Maids of Honor"

Over my head yards of taffeta tent;
night slides down.
The hoop wobbles into place.

I am a princess
in pretend brocade.
I have the Infanta's
porcelain nose
her salient eyes.
Stilled for that instant,
energy leaps
our strands of hair touch
pinned down with red blooms.
I am Margarita!
I raise my arm. A dwarf appears
and ladies-in-waiting.
In the mirror we bound.

Mama's pin pricks,
Velazquez winks. Mama wipes
blood off my skin.
"A sign, they will love you
at Louise's wedding."

Louise appears
on her second-floor balcony
raven haired.
She is my dark mirror.
"*Salaam*." She waves.
Her breasts bounce.
She lifts hair from her damp neck.

"The groom is older than her father."
Mama shakes her head.

I see the old man press his body
down on her, down,
break her open
with his crooked stick.

"No!
I don't want to be
in her wedding!"
I pull at my flower girl costume,
but am pinned in.
"She especially asked
for you."

"Louise! Louise!"
The bull-elephant voice of her Arab
father
bellows,
sands the house of my bones.

Her eyes darken.
She disappears.

Two weeks,
neighbors whisper,
"A dowry dispute."

I suspect Louise, some mischief.
Her eyes meet mine
as her laughter echoes Tehran.
I breathe in the whole sky.

The dress ready,
I am in the garden
by the pond, posing,
my hands on the hoop skirt,
a handkerchief in my right hand;
ribbons trail my hair.
Sun ripples the shine of taffeta
mirrored in the dark pond.

Papa snaps my photo.
I have no place to go…

transmigrate forty years,
across two continents,
hold the photo
in the same hand
that is not the same

within me
the glossy child
vibrates.

BULLS OF BABOLSAR

They block the hill, kick dust.
We have to pass them
Both coming and going to the Caspian Sea.
I pull my robe tighter.
"Don't run," Mama warns.
I walk backwards
eyeing their lowered horns.

At night my brothers whisper.
"I know Atyia wants me," Leo boasts.
"The way she sways in that tight
dress and her tits half out."
Inside his belly the bull charges.
"She's ready for me.
If it wasn't for her husband.
He has a gun."
Leo kicks his covers.

As I sleep mosquitoes needle
my breasts, sew my belly and thighs.
In the light Mama lifts my nightgown,
sees the violation of red bumps,
a field of passion flowers swelling
my tender skin. I cannot stop
scratching. Blood catches
under my nails.

MARY FREERICKS

COUSIN KACHIK, THE MAP MAKER, 1943

You whirl the world with one hand.
Russia narrows on the sphere,
spreads out on the map you pin
to the table. With one finger

you stop Iran. The globe wobbles.
I see outlines of countries, no names,
and the oceans still white.
Pink and blue shavings mound.

If I breathe they might fly off.
You are paring the delicate green point.
With cotton ball powdered you tint Iran
smooth. Paper cuffs keep countries clean.

Three mounds disappear inside Russia.
Rose dust lifts, hovers over Europe.
Both our breaths keep fallout from landing.
"Sun spots are growing," you warn Papa.

"There may be violent sun storms."
The sun's fires spin unknown spirals.
I focus on the two cities I know, Tabriz,
Tehran, and the desert road in between.

A safe sun sewn above the lion brandishing
a sword waves over Iran. A yellow hill is rising.
I reach for the bright ball. Your dark eyes lift.
Beyond the border I color with no boundaries.

BLUE WATERMELON

Storm troopers bruise Russia's border
into a deformed hand. You are precise,
print in each name. In the tropical garden
of our pension, the owner pulls aside

a huge leaf. I see the giant bloom
white waxy petals, purple markings
line the center. I learn its Russian name
as I learn the Persian names of cities.

"Orchedaya," "Babolsar." Before the year is out
I will cross half the world that spun
beneath Kachik's fingers. From the Persian Gulf,
through the Suez Canal, past the Rock of Gibraltar.

Bucking an Atlantic hurricane, I will arrive
in Boston Harbor. At P.S. 189 Miss Weinstein
rolls down the map in front of the sixth grade
class. "Now Mary will show us where she came from."

And I just stand there, unable to read
the English word, "Iran," unable to puzzle out an owl
shape. Miss Weinstein waits, the class waits,
and I wait, red heat through my cheeks.

Forty years and I still cannot read road maps,
get lost on dark streets, detours
leading to strange landscapes.
I cannot read black signs against the night sky.

Soon the optical fiber telescope will map
Galaxies in three dimensions. Distant clouds
of gas, dim stars, quasars, reveal their naked
shapes, luminous signals, glyphs of that first flash.

Already cartographers on computers blink boundaries,
Print 3D CAM maps as if they were the Creator.
At Woolworth's lifting the latest globe pressed
tight on a balloon, I can blow up the world.

PRAYER

Palm to palm my mother teaches me to pray
Leaning over my bed in the dark,
"Ia Bokaa ditia. Bokh moia sila."

I repeat her Russian prayer,
"Ia Bokha ditia. Bokh moia sila."
I am God's child. God is my strength.

The Armenian priest, *Der Hayr*,
unwraps the linen around a gold cross.
He holds the huge ornate cross
in front of my lips.

Worried about germs from all the other lips,
"Nyet!" Mama whispers in Russian,
"Don't kiss it." And I hold back.

"Asdvads asis," my father says in Armenian.
"If God be willing, we will go to Tehran.
We will go to Mazandaran. We will go to Babolsar."

Why can't we just go?
In Babolsar fever strikes Papa,
delirious he hits his hand against the wall.

I dream of a black box and pray,
"Dear God, let Papa live."
Mama prays, "Thy will be done."

GARDEN MINIATURES

1.

In the afternoon desert of our naps
the garden calls us. Leo signals.
Mama's breathing deepens.
We steal past her lifting blanket.

Her breath follows us above the sheet,
Down the dim stairwell, a warning.
The door swings. We escape.
The bright garden trumpets.

Figs and cherries so low
I open my mouth for the fruit.
Pails of water heat in sun.
Barefoot, my brothers leap.

My toe catches a pail. The water spills,
soles sting. In the shade of the bushes
we find dark beetles massed,
topping each other.

Leo pulls apart a mating pair,
the dazed two dizzy on his palm.
He tilts the precipice. Clear wings,
unexpected, save them.

Fingers sticky, Leo coaxes
the servant girl to play horsey.
Her fanny bumps as Leo rides, rides…
My brothers' laughter splashes up

inviting. Hands lower me into the murky
water. Peter thrashes, *"Okenh indzi!"*
His thin arms do not hold him.
I freeze against the algae lip.

Peter's last breath,
my brother drowned
or grew fins and swam away.
The water mounds.

Leo brings Peter up gulping
for breath. The curtain drawn,
Mama sleeps. Shivering
we look down from the edge.

2.

The rooster, the hens gather
at my feet. I am the goddess
of seeds. Wings lift to my steps.
My colonies group and regroup
Around me as I fling;
they peck.

Makhmoud comes with an axe. The hens
scatter, cackling. The one on the block
keeps an eye open as the axe falls.
The body bolts upright,
turns, turns,
topples.

With a can Leo cuts apart a live frog.
The body, the head stay still.
He slides the head back
trying it on the body.
But
it drops.

I run to the other end of the garden.
I am Robinson Crusoe on my own island.
I rule the forest and the waves.
I decree all creatures safe.
Under the honeysuckle arch,
I dodge bees.

3.

Waves hit. Papa holds me,
water splashes salt in my mouth.
I cry out. He lifts me with the waves.

Fever hits. The Caspian Sea
will not cool him,
our vacation cut short.

Three doctors shake their heads
as the fever climbs
Papa calls out and dies.

Mama takes me to the living room.
I see the wax body, feel the cold hand
that is no longer Papa.

BLUE WATERMELON

Relatives encircle me
around a table in the garden.
A dry handkerchief for Mama,
I slip away, hide behind a tree trunk,
hug the rough bark, shaking.

MARY FREERICKS

SMALL HOTEL IN KHORRAMSHAHR, 1945

Our airy room on the second floor
is the only one, an island
on the flat roof. From a window
Mama and I sketch palm trees, Arabs,

the Persian Gulf. I fill in turbans,
easy flowing robes, add a camel.
Air flaps are curtains,
like sails. Mama is taking us to America.

Our cargo ship is still at port.
The next morning I wake to a beautiful lizard.
Green and jasmine skin glides a mosaic.
Pointing above the door jamb I wake Mama.

She sits and cries out, "A snake!"
wakes Leo and Peter, "Get dressed!"
Under the snake, one by one,
Mama rushes us through the doorway.

We escape. "Our things, Leo!"
How can she motion him
into the snake's room?
No! But I am silent.

Unlatched suitcases bulge,
balance on a sea of hands
through the window. The snake slithers
onto the glass.

BLUE WATERMELON

"Kill it!" Mama screams.
Men with sticks surround it.
One is poking my snake.
I wish it would whip away.

"*Khanom*, we can't kill it.
All its relatives will come.
This hotel will be swarming."
Our downstairs room, an oven,

we flee into the hallway.
Men in bright underwear fan themselves
With newspapers and bow to *Khanom*.
Down here there is nothing to do,

but sweat.

MARY FREERICKS

ELLIS ISLAND, 1945

I dream: the doctor shakes his head,
         the guard pulls me from Mama
         sends me back to Iran   alone...

        JOLTED   AWAKE
     as   fts
        cabin   li
             DROPS
OCEAN UNHINGED   SPLITS
  pulls up   indigo ink
    on its side -   unbalanced   mountains

                ceiling tips
                ship sucked
                into chasm
                in that hollow
                    I hold
        metal bunk cuts my palms

            peter and I seasick,

        Leo feverish

                          for days
      taste of fear as vomit
                     hard to rinse.
      We walk on deck.
            Sunsets bring us closer,
     close the Atlantic gap.
     We whisper, "Ellis Island...
     Emik...

"As the Ile de France docked
Armistice Day, 1928," Mama adds.
From Goharik's lap   they pulled Emik,
                            locked him
                            in the infirmary.
Auntie Goharik pointed
           at the Statue of Liberty.
The guard from the garden at Ellis Island
answered, "Don't you see,
she has her back turned."
                        Emik deported, deported...

BLUE WATERMELON

A foghorn wakes me.　　　　　　　　　　　another nightmare.
Our Victory ship "VOOMS!"
All nine passengers on deck,
clumsy in close quarters
our cargo ship nears shore.

A tugboat turns us easily
spotting back.

My hand tightens in Mama's.
We point into the fog,
"Ellis Island?"

"This is Boston Harbor, Ma'am,"
a sailor says. "There's a dock strike
in New York."

My brothers and I shake; waves
of laughter wash out weeks
of fear. The anchor
drops. The floor is still.
I wind through ships
of muscled sailors,
an able tug.

Steady on American soil,
my legs adjust.
The customs inspector
searches our trunk
as our three uncles wait.
He lifts rosin, bow and violin,
lets us go!

"_Achikjan, inch bes ek?_"

FLIGHT

1.
The earth tilts,
the shying machine.
I grasp the one Mind; we bump.
My breath returns.
We're walking on air.

Papa gone.
Mama is taking us to
meet the ship for America
in a twin engine plane
crossing Iran,
approaching too close to the mountain,
wings bank.

2.
As I enter the Pacific,
tar catches my legs and feet.
We will not plunge
into a garden of fantasy,
following a rabbit,
holding keys to little doors
where transformation is normal
and tears build lakes.
Is that a cloud?
No, it is rising from the ground
and building like a volcano.

BLUE WATERMELON

Brackish water bubbles methane
and the tar, black islands
that did not hold the mammoth,
the terror trumpeting as hooves sink.
Before them the dinosaurs,
their bodies sank into tar,
float as some prehistoric ghosts
on a golden lake.

A cloud, an angel wing,
stretches into a specter,
an Iranian plane downed, on fire.

"Of course we care," Bush answers.

My husband's foot on the gas,
winged dinosaurs, their red bodies
take our sky away.

We are at the base of the Sierras.
The rented car curves up the mountain,
the low sun blinding,
Manzanita dry.
Fallen rock zones,
will the rockface buck?

In the dark you can see
the forest.
From the valley
I lift my head
and see the stars,
A covenant?

MARY FREERICKS

SADDI'S ANCIENT BOOK

The orange book opens. Agaa leafs
backwards. A stale odor rises
from the thick pages. I make out Persian
letters. But halfway within a word,
they change shape. I lose the sense.
I have forgotten the Persian I knew.

The columns must be poems.
I persuade him to read one, they flow
a familiar sound from my childhood.
He will not translate.
This is the time for his English lesson.
Zubada brings tea, kneels to help him
with his slipper on his swollen foot.

We stop at a picture of a lion
holding a sword, the *shir wa khurshid*.
He tells me, "Lion, milk, lamb,
Sun are all a form of *shir.*"

The mane has the same tight curls I felt
in the mountain pass. My brave fingers
reached the giant warrior's beard
on the bas-relief as I stood on my toes,
a thumb curving around the rough stone.

The sun on the lion's back wears a woman's face
as she rises sending rays from her head.
Is there a myth? Agaa is not ready to tell,
With his wife at his feet. He shakes his head.

BLUE WATERMELON

On the Persian flag someone has stripped the woman
off the lion's back. He rules alone with his
scimitar. The sun has lost its face.
She is hiding somewhere within the folds
of fabric. In the dark of the bedroom
she lets her *chador* fall and blazes.
The flag is a lesson in perception.

If you look at the flag long enough from within
the weave, you will see the woman sending rays
from her head. I see the pattern of ropes
behind the lion and sun. The earth, the sky
filled with lines of rope in Saddi's book.

Is this embroidery a sign of the beginning
before the separation of man and woman, of sky
and earth? Agaa closes the book.

MARY FREERICKS

I WILL RISE UP

I will rise up against my protectors.
Their kind eyes set stern towards me,
All my brothers and sisters who say, "No!"
They are a ring of columns that block
the angel cadets of my desire.
I see banners, red hair flying.
I hear trumpets.

I will dive through the air
into the ring of fire; arms
of cadets will hold my strapless body.
I am no village baby wrapped around
her mother's breasts. I will not suckle
'til my insides turn black.
I rip off the *chador*. I will not
be trained to use only one eye.
Safety falls at my feet.

I stand between the horns of two oxen.
My husband leaves the lens cap on.
His hands shake. My one moment of courage
unrecorded, fades.

I will board the helicopter
that has no doors.
I will ride the elephant.
I will walks the streets of slums.

I will spray courage musk
all over my body.
No one will dare stop me.
I will bristle on the high heels of courage.

NARGIZ MAMA'S PRAYER

I glanced over the guest. Uncle Alex was sitting in the stuffed chair by the window. I noticed the seat on the sofa next to him was empty. As I made my way toward him with a hot cup of tea in one hand and piece of cake in the other, he made room for me with a welcome smile that filled his round face.

"How are you, Mary?" he asked, rolling his "Rs" and taking another bite of cake.

"Fine," I answered, taking a sip of tea. This was my chance to ask him about Nargiz Mama.

The presents had all been opened and the guests served were chatting among themselves; the children playing in another room were running in and out.

The coffee cup looked fragile in his large hand as he took a final sip and placed it down. Then he leaned back in his chair, as if trying to sink back in time.

"Yes, she was your grandfather's mother. A wiry, courageous woman. She prayed every morning and every night without fail."

"Her prayers were like a regular exercise," said Uncle Vaughinak, who was sitting across from us on a piano bench leaning forward. "She kneeled all the way down to her forehead and got up to a standing position about ninety times as she asked for God's blessing."

"Did she pray for each member of the family?" I asked, surprised at the sudden recognition that my Uncle V resembled Nargiz Mama. His frame kept the unsteady bench from tipping.

"Yes, every single one, from the oldest down to the very youngest. One day I sneaked into the dining room doorway. I heard her praying. She was calling on 'Levon's God.'"

"She would start with your grandfather," Uncle Alex added, looking into my eyes. 'For Khosrov,'" she would say as she asked God's blessing, she would kneel down and rise again. "'For Alex who is far away serving in the Russian Army, God Bless him,'" all the way down to the youngest grandchild. She got up and kneeled each time, whispering her prayers out loud.

"Uncle V, tell me about your train accident when you were pulled under the tracks. Do you believe Nargiz Mama's prayers saved you?"

"Yes, Uncle Alex had some narrow escapes in the Russian Army too."

I looked at Uncle Alex. Neither uncle seemed ready to talk about himself.

"What about Levon?" I asked, deciding to bring in someone a little more remote. "I remember something about a grenade exploding in his hand. Is that how he lost, was it one or two fingers?" Levon's tall, debonair, prominent nose and dark flashy eyes went through my mind. He was now happily settled in Belgium, managing the family rug business there. The enamel pin of the steering wheel of the Queen Mary, which he had given me as a gift when I was in my teens, still lay in the top dresser drawer of my bureau. That was the last time I had seen Levon in this country.

I seemed to have hit the right key to open the secret of Nargiz Mama's power. Uncle Alex brightened. "Levon had another narrow escape when he was very young."

"Oh, I didn't know about that," I said. "Where were they living then?"

"Tiflis, in Georgia, a beautiful city. Must have been around 1917, the outbreak of the Russian Revolution.

"He was playing on the balcony of the apartment. The balcony was very high up, on the second floor. The way houses were built in those days, it was like three floors up. Levon jumped up on top of the banister playing horsey. He stood up on the banister, lost his balance and fell the wrong way onto the rough concrete below, a three-floor drop. The thud made the neighbor think one of the cases stored on the balcony had fallen. The family ran to see what happened. They found Levon lying unconscious. For twenty-four hours he remained unconscious."

"They found he had no injuries when he came to. The recovery from the accident was amazingly fast," Uncle V added.

"Do you believe Nargiz Mama's prayers protected Levon from serious injury?"

"Yes," they both answered. "Or even death," Uncle V added.

"Levon must have been around ten or twelve when the explosion occurred. After the Revolution explosives lay scattered here and there through the countryside. One had to be very careful. One day Levon was playing. He found a copper tube on the ground the size of a thin cigarette. Levon picked it up."

"He wanted to make a pencil cover out of it," Uncle V added.

"It was closed at one end," Uncle Alex continued. "He noticed some white powder in it and started to scrape the powder out 'til very little remained inside the tube. The powder was dynamite. Your cousin George, who was around four years old, was watching Levon. Matches were on the table. A fraction of a second before he brought the match up to the tube, George left the table. The violent explosion tore Levon's left hand apart, carrying off one or two phalanges of each finger except his little finger. The dynamite and the copper tube was probably some detonator used during the Revolution. If the powder had been left in the tube the full force of the exploding dynamite would have certainly killed him and possibly injured George. The chain of incidents was too unusual to be considered mere chance."

"They had to graft a piece from his stomach onto his hand, but this injury healed. Through natural adaptation the little finger developed in size and strength," Uncle V continued. By now some of the ladies were listening. "He can now use his left hand almost normally, for instance in sports and in the gym."

"He was part of the gymnastics team at Louvain University," Uncle Alex added. "In the summer of 1952 Levon had another miraculous escape from death. He was busy putting tennis equipment in the trunk of his car. He did not see a truck out of control. The truck crashed into him. The shape of his body was impressed into the rear fender of his car and he fell unconscious. When he came to at the hospital, he could not move. There was terrible pain all over his body, especially in his legs. His body was covered with severe bruises. He thought all his bones were smashed to pieces. The X-rays showed only one broken collar bone and a fractured pelvis.

"Surgery repaired the collar bone. He spent six weeks in bed at the hospital while the pelvis fracture healed. Then after a week of rest at home, they took X-rays again. Both fractures were perfectly healed. A month later Levon was out playing tennis, which as you know is a vigorous sport. Two months later he was at the gym vaulting on the horse."

I sat silent, amused by the multiplicity of the proof. I wished I had met my great grandmother. Perhaps I would have caught some of the fire of her faith – a faith the members of her family still felt even though she was now long dead.

I looked at Uncle V. He reminded my mother of Charles Boyer. He had given up smoking after his heart attack. "Tell me about your train accident. How old were you when it happened?"

"I was thirteen years old. The accident happened at Armavir. We were on the train traveling from Yessentuki in the North Caucasus. The whole family was moving to Rostov. All our packed goods were on the freight train."

"How long were you on the train before the accident?"

"We had already spent the night. The train was very long. A passenger train was attached to the back of the freight train. The freight train rode high from the ground. The passenger train rode very low to the ground. The train stopped at Armavir. I got out to stretch my legs and use the bathroom. When I came back the train was already moving. I ran to the platform. The train had no steps, just planks hanging on ropes. I put my foot on the plank and tried to get on. My father grabbed my hand as the train sped up. I lost my grip. I don't know exactly what happened next. Somehow I was thrown clear of the wheels as I felt myself pulled under the freight car. Stunned, I lay on the ties. Something kept hitting my head no matter how low I pulled myself. Dizzy with fear, I was partly conscious of my aching leg and throbbing head as the giant wheels rolled past."

"Why didn't somebody stop the train?" I asked.

"In those days there was no emergency cord. A man used to shoot a gun to stop the train.

"As the freight train roared over me, I knew any moment I might be cut in half by the approaching passenger train, which rode much lower to the ground. Somebody managed to pull me out just before the passenger train rode over the spot where I had been. He tore my shirt and wrapped it about my bloody head."

"What about the family in the speeding train?"

"My father rode back. He found me not only alive, but with minor injuries. A little iodine and clean bandages were applied at the first aid station. I thank God and Nargiz Mama to this day."

A quiet settled over the guests as they listened to Uncle V's story. Even the children sat hushed on the floor listening.

I looked at Uncle Alex. "What do you remember about Nargiz Mama?" I asked.

"She had beautiful expressive eyes. In her youth she must have been very attractive.

"We owned property in Salmast (Haftavan). When I was little like you boys, she would pick the strongest horse. She would put me on the back of the horse. Then we would ride through our large acreage as she examined the fields."

"She walked to church," Uncle V added. "Two, three miles, she walked, back and forth. When we lived in Rostov, the Armenian Church was in Nohima. Karapet, your great-grandfather Don would say, 'Nargiz, why do you walk to church? It's raining, why don't you take the trolley? It's cold.' 'No,' she would answer, 'I'll walk.' It was part of the sacrifice. No matter how cold, windy and snowy it got, she walked to church."

"She even walked during the Revolution, when they were shooting in the streets," Uncle Alex added.

"Those were terrible times," Mama said. "The military government sent soldiers to pick people up. Then they would shoot anybody who carried money on him or anything else wrong they might find. Just shoot people. Your papa had 5,000 in czarist currency. He was with another man. They were both very young. He was planning to exchange the money. The police were picking people up in the street for questioning. They arrested your papa and the other man. They took them to the station to wait for the interrogation, search, and then face the firing squad. Papa was big and strong, but what could he do against guns? He was terrified as he waited, and more people were brought in. He prayed intensely. He knew he had the money on him. If they searched him, they would execute him. There seemed to be no escape. Then he heard a voice commanding, "Let them go!" He couldn't believe his ears. He was released without being searched. He was free to live!

"The impression stayed with him the rest of his life. Papa never forgot the experience. That night they finally left secretly, even though Vaghoush had diphtheria."

"Nargiz Mama went on a pilgrimage to Jerusalem," Uncle V added. The children ran off to play, and separate conversations started around the room. "She visited all the sacred places. Vahram took her. He was never afraid after that. Even when he fought in World War One. 'She prayed for me,' he used to say. 'I feel safe since Nargiz Mama prayed for me.'"

"What about your experiences, Uncle Alex, were you at any time protected by Nargiz Mama's prayers?" I asked Uncle Alex.

"Since you ask me, I will tell you; although, I do not usually talk about it." I saw a faraway look in his eyes as he tried to recapture the event. "The Russian Regiment was staying in Astrakhan in southern Russia, bordering Persia near the Caspian Sea and the Southern Caucasus Mountains. The Turks with local Muslims were coming to throw us into the sea. With me there were two hundred soldiers."

"Were you in command?"

"Yes, I was a *Paruchik*," he thought for a moment, "Lieutenant. The main forces of the Russian Regiment were in front of the Turks. To confuse the Turks, two companies went behind the Turks and were cut off from the main force. Our company was one of those two. We planned to attack. It was too late. Turks surrounded us. They started shooting at us. There was cracking of rifles and the bursting of shells all around. My men fell with agonizing dying moans. A man five feet from me got a bullet in the stomach. One fellow lost his eyes.

"We were in an apple orchard, surrounded by the Turks. The rays of the sun shone through the branches on the floor of the garden. I looked at the sunny day and thought, 'This is not the time to die.'

"Suddenly I remembered grandma taking me to church early Easter morning. It was still dark when she woke me up. On the way, I revolted. 'I don't want to go,' I said, dragging my feet.

"'Let's go to church,' she coaxed, 'and pray to God.'

"'Who's God?' I asked.

"'God is only as far as your elbow,' she answered. That picture flashed in my mind as I stood in the apple orchard, with shells cracking all around.

"I took the gun of a dead soldier, raised it over my head, and shouted, 'Those who believe in God, come with me!'

"We attacked the Turks and cut them in two parts. The other company cut through to the main force in front of the Turks. The day was saved. To this day, I think that in the darkest part of life, the power of the Almighty works for our benefit."

Then I realized how well Uncle Alex had recovered from his stroke, and that the last time I called Auntie Goharik had answered the phone. She said, "No I can't get Uncle Alex right now. He's out mowing the back lawn."

What was this power Nargiz Mama possessed?

MOVING AWAY

(ESSAY WRITTEN AT AGE SIXTEEN)

When I had to move from Nyack, New York to Englewood, New Jersey, a distance of twenty miles, I knew that break would be a difficult one to make. Once before I had moved halfway across the world from Persia to the United States; yet this complete break with the familiar Asiatic culture and customs to a new and modern world of flashing lights, skyscrapers and a giant mass of moving cars did not affect me as much as moving the short distance of thirty minutes from a beautiful town overlooking the Hudson River to a city in the New York suburbs. Possibly the age difference can partly explain my reactions. When I moved from Persia I was eleven years old. I was fourteen when I moved from Nyack. Now, as I think back, I sometimes wonder how four years in the life of a young girl can make so much difference.

I had always looked forward to coming to America. The rest of the family were so eager to go that I shared their enthusiasm. My enthusiasm was marred by my father's death; yet I did not feel secure remaining in Persia without a man at the head of our family. Women are regarded as inferior beings in Persia. We are Christian Armenians. Since Persians are Mohammedans they hold a different view of life. Thus I never really felt that Persia was my motherland.

My uncles, who lived in America, had sent us a telegram shortly after my father's death, urging us to come to the United States.

We started making preparations to move. Often I would go to the American consulate with my mother while she tried to get a visa. My brothers were both quite excited. We began to sell our samovar, our china and our antique Louis XVI table to strange men for very poor prices.

One day my mother came in with a glowing yet slightly worried face.

"Children, come here," she said. "Darlings, I was told at the embassy that a ship is at port. We can take this ship from Khorramshahr. We must leave as soon as possible."

My heart leapt. "So we are really going?"

The next day there was a bus strike, one of the very rare ones ever held in Persia. Thus my older brother Leopold asked a friend with a car to drive Mama to the railroad station so she could buy tickets.

Due to a Muslim holiday, the railroad station was closed, and she was informed that all the trains leaving the next day were already filled up. Our only solution was to take an airplane. My mother signed for one. We were to fly the next morning to Khorramshahr.

My cousins, who lived across the street, came to visit us. Onik and Rafik, the two boys, were approximately Peter's and my age. Peter is my other brother. He is one and a half years older than I am and three years younger than Leopold. I had often played ping pong, chess, or soccer with Peter, Leopold, Onik, and Rafik. I loved both my cousins; yet, possibly because I always wanted a girl friend, the thought of leaving them did not hurt me. We exchanged promises to write letters, promises I never kept.

Soon after my cousins left, Marina, my best friend, dropped in to say good-bye. With Marina I had often played house, feeding and dressing my large cloth doll that had a pointed nose, which my mother had sewn. Boys thought playing with dolls was sissy. Of course I promised to write to Marina. A year later, I remember sending her a Christmas card with apologies of why I had not written previously. By then I had forgotten most of my Persian and writing from right to left seemed odd.

The next morning it was still dark when we arose. We reached the airport in the cool dawn. A small, two-motor, silver plane started to purr. My great aunt Khourik had tears in her eyes. As all the relatives kissed me good-bye, I felt a little sad. Was I never to see these familiar faces again? I shook hands with Onik and Rafik and was helped up to the plane.

"Dear, let me show you how to fasten your seat belt," my mother's soft arm helped me into the seat.

I felt a little panicky as the plane started to circle the field. This was my first flight. The plane started to rise.

"We're flying, Mama! I don't feel any different."

My brothers started walking around in the plane.

"Look! We can walk on air," they shouted.

I looked around the deep clear blue sky and far down at the midget trees. The full meaning of completely leaving all my friends and relatives did not touch me. I was secure and happy with my two brothers and my mother.

When we reached Khorramshahr, the American embassy

informed us that we would have to wait two weeks before we could get on the ship. Even in September Khorramshahr is intensely hot. As I walked down the street, I would tighten the hold on my mother's warm, moist hand under the stare of Arabs with high turbans.

Inside the small square hotel room where the only window was draped with heavy curtains, I would lie on the bed soaked with perspiration in the oppressive noon heat. I hated just waiting in Khorramshahr. I was eager to get on the ship. At times I even wished I were home again, eating grapes in the cool garden protected by high walls at twilight.

Finally we were asked to get on the ship. A jolly sailor helped me up the rope ladder and on to the hot steel ship. Later he offered me a peppermint Life Saver. As the ship got into motion, I felt a cool sea breeze.

We were on a cargo ship carrying approximately fifteen passengers because of the scarcity of passenger ships right after the war. There were only three females on the ship, a twenty-eight-year-old woman, my mother and me. All the sailors were very friendly. As I sat up on deck, a sailor below deck would shout, "Where's the little girl?"

The magazines and Life Savers would fly up into my lap.

The captain, a forty-year-old ruddy-faced man, called me his sweetheart. He fed me ice cream and dates.

I did not enjoy every minute of the trip. The rocking of the ship turned my stomach, and I had trouble getting used to American food. Peanut butter and jelly sandwiches, tomato juice, and greasy potatoes did not agree with me. We ate with the officers. An old Swedish engineer always amused me. In stormy weather, he would tip his soup plate against the rocking of the ship and eat spoonfuls at the same time.

Sitting on a deck chair in the warm sun, I would gaze at the rolling waves and wonder what life in the United States would be like. Sometimes a pang of fear would enter my heart as I would think of Ellis Island. I was afraid of the doctors peering at me and listening to my thumping heart. I was a rather frail girl with a tint of yellow creeping into my cheeks from constant contact with the dry hot sun. What if they kept my mother and sent me back? I knew Mama would return with me, but I did not want to go back to Persia. Persia was a backward nation with few opportunities. I wanted to live in modern America. From contact with American soldiers stationed in Persia and with missionary children, I was certain I would like Americans.

Luckily, because of a sailors' strike we landed in Boston instead of New York. I did not have to go to Ellis Island. As I looked at the navy blue buildings rising in the foggy dusk, I felt both happy and sad. We were here at last, but what would this new strange country be like? Could I make myself understood with the little English I had learned from visiting American soldiers?

Then my mother nudged me. "There are your three uncles on the shore. Wave to them."

As I looked at the kindly faces they seemed familiar. Soon my uncles were on the boat kissing me. This was just like home.

For six months I lived with a younger cousin who spoke only in English. Soon I could talk to her fluently. I began to think in English and forget Persian.

I considered my break from Persian unimportant in comparison with my later move from one American city to another.

By the time I was in eighth grade living in Nyack, New York, I felt like an American girl with foreign parents. The thing I missed most, and still do, is Persian food. I would think of the bowls of hot fluffy rice, the stuffed grape leaves covered with yogurt, or the cool red water made from rose petals.

In Nyack I was socially accepted. My best friend was a peppy redhead, Audrey Arnold. Audrey's pinkish, pale skin was covered with freckles. I enjoyed teasing her about having red eyes, for her eyes were exactly the same color as her curly hair. Often she would wear a shade of green or turquoise to accentuate her hair. We loved to skip around in the schoolyard, jump rope or whisper secrets. Our bald history teacher, Sammy Templin, called us Siamese twins.

I was popular among the other girls and boys. At a dance given by the Tri-Y of which I was a member, I danced with every boy there except two boys who had come with dates. When I was awarded the American Legion medal for good citizenship, I was filled with happiness to think that the boys and girls had voted for me.

Then came the blow. My older brother was attending Juilliard in New York City every Saturday. The next year he would be going five days a week; we had to move closer to New York. Otherwise he would lose too many practice hours because of the long bus trip. Leopold wanted to be a famous violinist. I realized that I should not stand in the way of his ambition, but I did not want to leave Nyack.

Nyack is such a beautiful town. Our alma mater describes it so well: "Nestled in the Hudson Valley, 'midst the mountains grand." Nyack is an old Indian name for queen. I loved the large protecting trees and glistening blue river, but most of all I loved popularity. I did not want to go to a new city where no one would recognize me. I would have no one to play with or to share my secrets.

It was the last day of school when I was certain we were leaving and had to tell my friends.

On a walk around the schoolyard with Audrey and another friend I said to Audrey, "We're moving away."

"You are? Where to?" Her voice was cold and mechanical.

The other girl said, "Oh, I'll miss you."

But Audrey was the one who should miss me. We were such good friends. I was startled and hurt. We promised to write to each other.

When the other boys and girls found out I was leaving they showered me with questions and affection. Secretly I had hoped for a surprise going away party, but I knew it was too late.

The weekend we were packing to move, I was invited to my uncle's house. When they brought me back, my uncle drove to Englewood instead of Nyack. I felt strangely sad not driving along the Hudson River to Nyack. We were riding on unfamiliar streets and asking for directions. Would I ever get home? As we entered Englewood, I was pleased by the wide avenue and the large five and ten. When I first saw the red brick apartments we had moved into, I was disappointed at finding only one scrawny young tree on the front lawn. Little running and screaming children covered the rest of the lawn. In the interior, I was struck by the bare walls. Most of our belongings were stacked up in cardboard boxes on the floor.

In a week the interior looked much better. We spread Persian rugs on the floor. The rug covering the living room floor had a delicate design dominated by soft rose-colored flowers. A soft gray couch was placed in between the two windows. Next to the couch was a lamp with a yellow-green lampshade. The armchair diagonally across the room carried out the same yellow-green, which contrasted with the deep cool green of the walls and the warm rose of the armchair in the opposite corner. A piano against the left wall was a dark brown, as dark as the little table covered with glass in front of the couch.

When the table and chairs of the dinette arrived, we were startled to find that mistakenly they had sent us a red table and yellow chairs. The combination seemed charming, but it looked ultra-modern and we decided to keep the table.

Visiting friends complimented us on our excellent choice of furniture.

All that summer I was very lonely. I would get so tired of listening to Leopold practicing exercises on his violin on hot humid days that I would go out and play with the children. I knew no girls my own age.

When I received a letter from Audrey, the glow of my former happiness returned. I answered her and corresponded with a few of my other friends.

When I registered in junior high school in September, I was asked whether I wanted to take science or Latin. This question seemed perfectly innocent. I did not know that 9/2 was the smartest Latin class and contained the core of the popular students in junior high. I chose science and was placed in 9/1, the smartest science class. The majority of the boys in 9/1 did not date. Many of them were good looking and fun, but when a school dance was given they stayed home while the 9/2 boys took the 9/2 girls, but the girls in 9/1 were jealous and said anyone who went around with them was trying to get into the clique. Thus, stupidly and shyly, I kept away from 9/2 and was a very unhappy person. I began to miss Nyack.

"If only I were in Nyack, I would be asked to all the dances," I would complain to my mother.

As months went by, I began to get acquainted with the people in 9/2, and I liked them. I had many friends, yet no one could take Audrey's place. I almost won the American Legion medal again at ninth grade graduation. I even got to go to the prom, although a 9/1 boy timidly asked me a day before the dance.

Later, in high school, I was fairly happy, but without extrovert Audrey gathering friends about, I had to work on my own. Often I was too shy to start a conversation with a boy. I became more of a student than I would have been had I continued to live in Nyack. Of course I went out on dates and to dances. Whenever I did miss a dance, I thought that if only I were in Nyack I would've been asked.

The break from Nyack in the long run had little effect on my life except a few unhappy years; yet when I moved only twenty miles, I felt the sharp cutting of friendships. The complete move from an ancient Asiatic country, Persia, hardly affected me emotionally. Now I realize that living in America has completely altered my life. In Persia I would most probably be a married woman by now, leading a narrow life and considering myself an inferior creature. In America I am an independent person going to college and preparing myself for a deeper understanding of life.

FOREIGN WORDS AND PHRASES

Aghkikjan – Armenian, sweet girl (dear girl)

Asdvadz asis – Armenian, God says

Atalakan kaaki – Arabic, eat cake

Byoushki, bayhou. bayhou– Russian, hush little baby

Baleh chashm – Persian, yes (literally, to my eye)

Bokh moia sila – Russian, God is my strength

Chador – Persian, head to foot veil

Der Hayr – Armenian, father (referring to priest)

Dolma – Armenian, stuffed grape leaves

Dushichka – Russian, darling soul

Ghadahafez – Persian, goodbye (literally, God be with you)

H'Ramatzek- Armenia, a toast used when drinking, "to your health"

Harik – Armenian, grandfather

Harss – Armenian, bride

Harsses – Armenian, brides

Heemar takoohi – Armenian, stupid queen

Inch bes ek – Armenian, how are you?

Ia Bokha Ditia – Russian, I am God's child

Kefta – Arabic, seasoned ground meat dish

Keta – Armenian, sweet breakfast roll

Khanom – Persian, Mrs.

Khelok takavor – Armenian, clever king

Khourik – Armenian, sister (name we called my grandfather's sister)

Kiaban – Persian, avenue (wide street)

Kohdah Hafez – Persian, good bye, but actually means "God be with you."

Lahmajune – Armenian, meat pizza

Lastichka – Russian, darling little bird

Lavosh – Armenian, flat bread without yeast, shaped like a pizza

Madzoon apour – Armenian, hot yogurt soup

Mariam Astvatsatsiny – Armenian, The Virgin Mary

Meykhane – Persian, after the advent of Islam the taverns run by Zoroastrians. Such taverns were considered sacred places that poets frequented.

Modir – Persian, principal

Moia zhena – Russian, my wife

Moomichka - Russian, darling girl

Nyet – Russian, no

Paron – Armenian, Mr.

Okenh indzi – Armenian, help me

Orchedaya – Russian, orchid

Salaam – Arabic, peace

Sangak – Persian, thick flat bread shaped like a Sicilian pizza

Sieg Heil – German, To Victory

Shahies – Persian, 1/100th of a dinar (less than a penny)

Sheru kurshid – Persian, the lion and the sun

Spi molodetskaia moia prekrasnaia – Russian, sleep my beautiful baby

Tikin – Armenian, Mrs.

Tonir – Armenian – bread oven, a hole in the ground with brick walls and a hot fire at the bottom

Tour Inds Me Patrchik – Armenian, give me a kiss

Ya Maskvitchkaya– Russian, I'm from Moscow

Zdravstvuyzte – Russian, hello, literally "to your health"

BLUE WATERMELON

ABOUT THE AUTHOR

Mary Freericks is a prize winning poet with magazines in dozens of publications across the world including the New York Quarterly, Cosmopolitan, and the Christian Science Monitor. She has also appeared in many anthologies including To Give Life A Shape edited by David Starkey and Chryss Yost, For She is the Tree of Life, edited by Valerie Kack-Brice, Poetry in the Garden edited by Jaqueline Miller, Armenian-American Poets, a bilingual, anthology edited by Lorne Shirinian.

Her writing is authentic, intense, textured with multicultural memories.

Mary has taught poetry both for the New Jersey State Council on the Arts and California Poet in the Schools as well as in service course to teachers in both states. She has led workshops for the Geraldine R. Dodge Poetry Festival.

Her poetry readings include Distinguished Poets Series, William Carlos Williams Poetry Center, International Women's Writers, Armenian Students' Assoc. held at Princeton University, Karpeles Manuscript Library, and School of Creative Studies UCSB.

Among her many awards are the Allen Ginsberg Poetry Award and Distinguished Achievement Award for Excellence in Photojournalism.

She has taught at Santa Barbara City College, Ventura College, Fairleigh Dickinson University, and Bergen Community College. She has appeared in film, television and radio.

Made in the USA
San Bernardino, CA
20 January 2018